I0505588

© Law Cheuk Yui / Michael Andrew Law. All Rights Reserved.

Michael Andrew Law
Artist Statement
「藝術家自述」

My paintings tries to captured the Soul of Youth , I combines classical mediums such as Pigment & Oil with contemporary painting method and medium such as Digital CG as Giclée Prints , I Only interested on ONE but immortal subject matters : Female Figures, by set against the figures with chinese calligraphy Employing the Idea of Word as Image, as an expressive scenario . I use both Life models and Computer Generated Images for the creation of works .

Through juxtaposition, both Icons (The Words and Female figures) , Both added meanings to the other.

These paintings are My Own interpret and to document HongKong's own Millennial and its Generation's view point and identities : As "Hongkonger".

oil on canvas 30x30″

oil on canvas 32x46″

oil on canvas 9x4′

Michael Andrew Law at Work.

Michael Andrew Law

Michael Andrew Law (Born Law Cheuk Yui) was born 1982 in British Hong Kong. After studying Classical oil painting private lessons with New York Artist Daniel Anderson (1928 - 2008) at the his then-new workshop in Hong Kong, he made a stunning reputation as the designer of a number of cover spreads for the press in Hong Kong and abroad and as an illustrator and creative designer of various Comic Books / Story Books .

He then stepped away from commercial work and devoted himself solely to Oil painting. In recent years, he has aesthetically moved away from a stylistic "Icons Photorealist" to HongKonger-Realism, pushing his rendered subjects into a mythological arena. His artistic visions are treasured and collected by many . From there, Law quickly gained recognition in the art world by exhibiting at Hong Kong Convention and Exhibition Centre , The Avenue of Stars ; Law′s works are also appreciated and collected by many Hong Kong and international collectors.

Some of Law's Religious artworks for Catholic Church of Hong Kong are also gained media attention in 2006 and 2007 ,and was also received by the Cardinal of the Catholic Church in the same year .

His Pale Hair Girls are a thoroughly subversive tribute to the world of appearances worshipers and to the Hong Kong's Millennial Generation culture of 21 century, with which the painter has cultivated an almost ritualistic relationship. His paintings provoke and compel. There is a unique realness in spirit.

The artist lives and works at Central District , Hong Kong.

Solo Show at NatureArt Gallery

At Ceremony with the Cardinal

Michael Andrew Law

(852) 6444-7550

info@michaelandrewlaw.com

www.michaelandrewlaw.com

HONORS AND AWARDS:

*Medici Cast Study Recognized by Social Fine Arts Grade Examination Center Of China Academy Of Art.
*Social Fine Arts Grade Examination Center Of China Academy Of Art Promotional Art(2011-present)
Publishers Weekly Best illustrated 's Coffe Book 2004 (Pete M.Parks)
The Salt and The Light Catholic Church Children Book 2004 (Mars)
Borders Magazine Most Original Voices nominee 2006 (Dear Fish)
Publisher's Weekly Best Children's Book list 2004 (America the Beautiful)
Communication Digital Artist -- Award of Excellence
European Print Weekly Design Annual Awards (2000,2002)
Face to face Dolphin art competition silver award 2006
Art Directors of HKC Award of Merit (2005)
Society of Fine Art -- An exhibitor 2005 Society of Newspaper Design Award of Excellence
Michael and Stephanie Duo Exhibition (2006)
Spectrum Fantastic Art Annual (multiple)
not-for-profit aution for Rotary of HK 2012

Art Funtion for
Organic Beauty opening

Exhibition :

2013 DeTour Matters 2013 Satellite Events at NatureArt Gallery
2013 December to Remember , One man show at NatureArt Gallery Central District, Hong Kong.
2012 Solo Show , Park Central tseung kwan O ,Hong Kong
2011 Art Walk Group Showing , Discovery Bay ,Hong Kong
2011 HK Gold Coast (Book signing exhibition)
2009 Solo Painting Exhibition The Avenue of Stars
Group Exhibition of Daniel Anderson workshop Classical Realism class of 2008 at Manhattan,NY
2007 Guest and ExhibitionThe Peak Galleria Hong Kong
2007 invited workshop exhibition, Elements, Hong Kong
Group Exhibition of Classical Realism class of 2007 at Manhattan,NY
2006 Collection by Cardinal Zen Ze-kiun and exhibited at Catholic Church of Hong Kong.
2004 - 2007, Hong Kong Young Artist Group Exhibition, Hong Kong Central Library.
Group Exhibition of Classical Realism class of 2006 at East Village, Manhattan,NY
2005 Illustration original exhibition for Kung Kao Po
2004 Group Exhibition, Wanchai Tower
2003 Group Exhibition, Hong Kong Convention and Exhibition Centre.
2003 Winner of i luv Hong Kong Painting Competition, exhibition at The Landmark (Hong Kong).
2002 The Holy story Picture Book illustrated picture original exhibition ,sai wan ho civic centre.

Art Funtion at
The Peninsula Hong Kong

SELECTED COLLECTIONS :

Cardinal of the Catholic Church Joseph Zen Ze-kiun
Organic Beauty Inc
Agriculture, Fisheries and Conservation Department
Ms.Ho Wei Ying
Ms. Annie Yu
Daniel Anderson
MR.Tsang Yan Sam

Interview with Hollywood Film
Producer / Teacher Dov Simens

PUBLICATIONS :

Fisheye magazine , featured artist interview , November 2002 (ISBN: N/A)
Kung Kao Po , interview , June 2006 (ISBN: N/A)
Art of Rock Realism , 2008 (ISBN: N/A)
Michael Andrew Law Early works Volume 1 - 3 :
(ISBN-13: 978-1503319400)
(ISBN-13: 978-1503366060)
(ISBN-13: 978-1503365087)
The Pale Hair Girls of Michael Andrew Law , 2010 (ISBN-13: 9781503372115)
December to Remember One man Show Art Book , 2013 (ISBN-13: 9781505609257)
Christmas Everyday : Pale Hair Girls Christmas Series 1 (ISBN-13: 978-1505453218)
Christmas Everyday : Pale Hair Girls Christmas Series 2 (ISBN-13: 978-1505467796)
Christmas Everyday : Pale Hair Girls Christmas Series 3 (ISBN-13: 978-1505468052)
Christmas Everyday : Pale Hair Girls Christmas Series 4 (ISBN-13: 978-1505470741)
Christmas Everyday : Pale Hair Girls Christmas Series 5 (ISBN-13: 978-1505470857)
Christmas Everyday : Pale Hair Girls Christmas Series 6 (ISBN-13: 978-1505471151)
Christmas Everyday : Pale Hair Girls Christmas Series Specials (ISBN-13: 978-1505583922)
i-Egoism by Michael Andrew Law (ISBN:978-1-4990-2124-0)

Exhibition at
Hong Kong Central Library.

Group Exhibition at
Hong Kong Museum of Art

Exhibition at Avenue of Stars, Hong Kong (2010)

Exhibition at Hong Kong
Convention and Exhibition Centre.

關於藝術家MICHAEL ANDREW LAW:

生長於交接時期香港的年輕藝術家 Michael Andrew Law，擅長把數碼繪圖，Pop 摩登藝術及古典油畫揉合時事及諷刺，創出獨特的視覺藝術語言及內容，跨越中西混合背景思維界限，探索互聯網世代交錯回歸的中西混雜之香港歷史。

他以自由隨意的手法結合摩登及古典材料與技巧，保持表現與認知、控制與隨性、魯莽與機智、自我與社羣等對立美學力量之間的張力，並對香港Y世代、本土文化及民族社會的殘酷現實作出尖刻的評論。Michael Andrew Law 的作品色彩豐富，寫實風格描繪的冰山美人，刻畫在滿佈流行文化圖像、東方書法標誌及符號的背景上。《白髮女孩糸列》(The Pale Hair Girls，2006 — 2013 年) 的創作之中，Michael Andrew Law 獨特的繪畫風格呈獻出達達主義思考方式般的出人意表的效果。畫中冰山美人式的人物穿插在抽象的香港和俗世號上。

Pale Hair Girls糸列的畫作的視覺靈感大量源自法國美術學院派大師William-Adolphe Bouguereau 的少年油畫作品以及已故華裔畫家陳逸飛的史詩及美人作品，Michael Andrew Law一反傳統的繪畫技法，以數碼混合古典繪畫技，重新演繹細緻複雜的中西方古典畫面和精心纖細思考的構圖，以西式媒介呼應中國的傳統書法裡作為圖案之筆觸，在Michael Andrew Law的筆下這種交錯西式POP ART和中式古典藝術表現時輪廓卻非常細緻，尤其最廣為流傳和臨摹的Leonardo da Vinci作品Mona Lisa (1517 年)，以東方血統之妻子肖像取代Mona Lisa 的表徵意義，極具質感的厚顏料同時呈現寫生畫作時人物肉體的細微變化。

《雖會理會不是自已的新天地:三聯畫》（Humanity）刻畫了在世代末日的未來世代們於本為廢墟的香港島上，等待著他們的命運。這些離奇的場景與 Jerry B. Jenkins及Timothy LaHaye等當代作家描寫的超現實、宗教解讀、未來主義情懷如出一致。於半島酒店扶輪會演講當代藝術

主要探索他藝術裡其中一項最重要的二分法：浪漫與嘲諷、作為藝術家對美的浪漫思者與交滙中西混合背景思維之香港Y世代的悲情，由天真燦爛的冰山美人式少女與可怕的末日和俗物之間的強烈對比作象徵。無論是標誌性的單幅「古典書法圖案的無身份肖像」，抑或以三聯畫形式出現，運用到大師級繪畫與構圖技巧，揉合了精細傳統油畫技法與摩登畫的表現方式建構，美人亦在美術史和流行文化裡是永恆的主題。冰山美人式少女令人聯想到生命的脆弱與時光飛逝之無情。藝術家就是要了解不同世界之間的界線並翻譯到不同文化價值之間的語境如高尚對低俗、古代對現代、東方對西方。

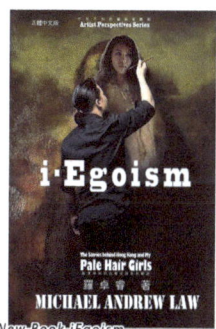

New Book iEgoism
ISBN:978-1-4990-2124-0

憑著 iEgoism 故事性的風格和精神，Michael Andrew Law將流行、古典與時事內容混合成一種感覺超豐富的視覺藝術作品，所涉獵的美學領域和文化靈感不斷延伸，而他在當中游走自如。一如常見的當代藝術主題，去作為「諷刺」及「反思」有關「浪漫」與「悲情」的直接敘述。

他所開發的iEgoism主題，就深受當代或反傳統藝術愛好者的喜愛，逼被視為跟西方DADA藝術主義互相呼應。Michael Andrew Law把自己置身於他熱烈的自我網世代主義- iEgoism裡展現出的姿態卻是完全屬於他本人和他的時代的。

Michael Andrew Law於2006 年隨美國紐約藝術家Daniel Anderson深造古典油畫，其後發展純美術繪畫工作，2008年獲贊助於香港中環成立藝術工作室 Nature Art。除了製作藝術及相關作品，Nature Art 及 Michael Andrew Law 亦積極培育香港年輕藝術家。

2013 年，他於NatureArt Gallery舉行藝術展覽《iEgoism》，從香港歷史中追溯當代香港流行視覺藝術文化的特徵。

Michael Andrew Law 的作品曾於紐約 Chelsea 的聯合展覽中展出，他亦曾在著名機構及學校舉行個展及講座，例如星光大道 (2009 年)、天主教香港教區、香港中央圖書館(2004 -2007 年)、灣仔政府大樓外 (2004 年)，香港會議展覽中心 (2003 年)。2015出版藝術文字著作《不可不知的藝術家觀點系列-iEgoism》更深入探討香港Y世代、香港歷史和Michael Andrew Law的作品脈絡關聯。

Michael Andrew Law 現於香港定居及從事創作。

Michael Andrew Law fusing digital and classical painting with west and East creative philosophy , to produce an extremely original artistic language and content that bridged west and east ,classical and modern medium , at the same time clearly tells the stories of his own generation. Combining digital creative materials and classical painting techniques with effusive yet knowing and precise focused , his paintings maintain a powerful tension between opposing aesthetic forces—expression and knowledge, control and spontaneity, savagery and wit, urbanity and primitivism—while providing satiric commentary on the oppressive realities of the predicament of Generation Internet, homegrown hongkonger's local-culture vesus Traditional Chinese culture, and The Hong Kong's post-handover history.

In his dynamically designed compositions, gracefully detailed figures and innocent faces are incise against fields that juxtaposed with portraits, chinese calligraphy, and sometimes cgi. The Pale Hair Girls Series (2006 - 2013) depicts realistic cold, icy-like young female figures surrounded by abstract and expressively painted forms and shapes revealing images of Pop culture, Historial figures, and Hong Kong landmarks.

Michael Andrew Law draws inspiration from Old Master's works such as Caravaggio , Ruben , Rembrandt , all the way to the Modern Art Superstars such as Warhol , Lichtenstein , Richter , De Kooning , Bacon , Wool and Prince . The Pale Hair Girls series mainly inspired by the painting works of French academic painter and traditionalist William-Adolphe Bouguereau and the Late Great YiFei Chen's characteristic "Romantic Realism" paintings.

In a reversal of standard East-West aesthetics, Law re-interprets Old Master's sophisticated imagery combine classical and digital materials—which resonate with Digital Vector Designs and Paintings—with fine strokes of oil paint multi-layered with paint film.In his interpretation of Leonardo Da Vinci's iconic Mona Lisa's smile (1517)—an iconic image that has been endlessly disseminated and reproduced—Law painted over the symbolism of the portrait Mona Lisa with his young wife , intent on rendering the figure in contemporary fashion with the iconic image as background .

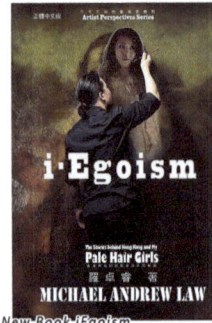

New Book iEgoism
ISBN:978-1-4990-2124-0

"The Humanity triptych" depicts New Generation HongKongers in a Ruined Hong Kong city , awaiting their unknown fate of a new beginning. This painting series explores one of the central paradox of his art—between romance and derision , his romantic magnanimity as an artist and his pessimistic perspective on the predicament of Generation Y Hongkongers. Here, this paradox is symbolized by the stark contrast of icy cold young female and disturbing representations of the armageddon-like of images. Whether portrayed as single "chinese calligraphy " or in triptych composition and classical paintwork that combine both expressive and traditional painting techniques with the digital vector , the beauties and the human figures stand as eternal motifs in the history of art and also in popular culture. Both oppositional and parallel, they are reminders of the fragile vibrancy of life and the impitoyable passing of time.

A references between different cultural refrence (high/pop, classical/contemporary, east/west), Michael Andrew Law has stated that an artist should be someone who understood how to hybrid between different worlds and go ahead makes an effort to knowing them. With his distinctive "iEgoism" philosophy , which employs highly refined academic painting techniques to depict a mixture of abstract expressionism in a representational pop culture images. These techniques parallel to the themes of romance and predicament of this generation , he recollects and revitalizes narratives of irony and introspection.

Michael Andrew Lawwas born in 1982 in British Hong Kong , studied fine art with american artist Daniel Anderson and graduate of China Central Academy of Fine Arts Sam Zeng from 2003 - 2006 . He co-founded the Hong Kong Art Studio Nature Art Workshop in 2008. In addition to the production and marketing of Michael Andrew Law's art and related work, Nature Art functions as a supportive environment for the fostering of emerging Hong Konger artists. Law is also a curator. In 2013, he organized an exhibition of contemporary art titled "iEgoism ," which served as a narration of contemporary HongKong Gen Y pop culture .

談所謂偽君子:
先說我寫這篇文並不是完全出於怒憤,也只是當是得啖笑的一則記綠我想法的文章吧。

若說有人討厭我的作品,在近幾年我根本不介懷,反之更暗暗高興,這是在藝術界打滾了這麼多年學到的,就是那怕是有觀眾討厭我的作品,還是愛死我的作品,至少觀眾已在不同程度地受我的作品影响吧。

先說藝術家要做的和一個科學家也很接近就是大家也要在既有的以外去探索,也是因此藝術家才對文明進步如此重要,就是先以身涉險的去找新的想法和可能性,然後告訴大家"往這個新空間想一想其實也可能不錯吧"的訊息。
遺憾是在香港的藝術教育直至幾年前還停留於藝術就是糊里糊塗的興趣班,藝術家就是不務正業的人。
可笑的是,當「大眾」在國際上因搞這些不務正業的事件而又因此賺了比起炒樓還要多時,就會先呆了並嘆其填""真幸運""然後想,這些"興趣"也許也要去玩玩,不致被同輩笑脫節吧。
不幸的是,在這些「大眾」心目中,仍只是因為是錢和同輩壓力才勉強接受藝術是"可能有用的東西",但因為多年來積累的"藝術就是糊里糊塗"的心態是沒變的,所以在「大眾」心中,就只有新聞上,雜誌上評為"珍品","天價品"才是藝術品 ,因為那些很值錢,那怕真的是糊里糊塗的東西,租個貴一貴的展廳，在場中掛得好，再在巴士站放廣告，就成了感覺上是「大眾」也買不起的"珍品"。

所以當一個藝術家，真的以"在既有的以外去探索"的精神去做時，大部份「大眾」是沒有足夠的知識去理解，但是在我的角度是，這種「大眾」再細分，還可分類為"可教育"和"不能教育"者。

還好的是"可教育"的人，只要藝術家真的是能夠証明自已的理念，而花功夫去翻譯給這些"可教育"的觀眾，他們還是能從以"在既有的以外去探索"的精神去學習欣賞。

而"不能教育"者，則是大概是上者的相反吧，情況在那些很看重框框的人身上就尤其明顯，只要作品不符這類人心目中所謂好作品的"典型"，不合"典型"的因素亦因人各異，通常他們連藝術家的解釋也懶的去聽。

說到如此，也許讀者以為我討厭"不能教育"者，反之，這幾年我學到的，就是以上所有各類觀眾也是我的目標對像，也許不是全部也是潛在客戶，但各類的觀眾卻同樣能驗証作品的"探索"指數。

當然，也不得不在此說，即使是那種觀眾，也可以討厭我的作

品，或愛死我的作品，是沒必然關系的，不
是說不喜歡我的畫就是"不能教育"者 ，但分別卻在於，"不能
教育"者是不會把"在既有的以外去探索"放在思路當中，在這種
人眼光中就只有"典型"和非"典型"，界線亦是根據喜好自定，
只要藝術家或作品"違反"了這種人"典型"的界線就休想說服他
們吧，尤其通常這種人以為自已已經知識廣博或是高尚道德標
準；最有趣是即使你引經據典，說明作品理念的依據，也是對
牛彈琴，是一項有趣的反智行為。

其實，也沒問題，我是很理解的；而寫了這個也許不會改變甚
麼，但反正要出書，就不要那麼多保留了；其實也已寫得很含
蓄；只是抒發一下觀察到的一個對反智行為，。

然而，我寫這的新書和這篇文章，我也視為我的藝術作品系列
中的一部份，有人會同意，有人會不同意，也顧不了這麼多。

順便送上一段金句:
『你們不要論斷人，免得你們被論斷。因為你們怎樣論斷人，
也必怎樣被論斷。你們用甚麼量器量給人，也必用甚麼量器量
給你們。為甚麼看見你弟兄眼中有刺，卻不想自己眼中有梁木
呢？你自己眼中有梁木，怎能對你弟兄說，容我去掉你眼中的
刺呢？你這假冒為善的人，先去掉自己眼中的梁木，然後才能
看得清楚，去掉你弟兄眼中的刺。』（太7:1-5）

引用毛主席，沒有作調查，就不該有發言權，無知未必是一種罪惡，但無知又要胡說八道者卻另作別論，多看看美術史，再看看William Bouguereau ，會田誠，Jeff Koons，Tracey Emin，Andres Serrano，Gustav Klimt，Marcus Harvey，甚至是當代天價級色情畫畫家John Currin；先理解甚麼是禁忌，甚麼不是禁忌，甚麼是藝術，甚麼不是藝術，甚麼是挑戰禁忌，甚麼是探索，連這些也未搞清楚，就只是瞎說罷了。

Michael Andrew Law

(852) 6444-7550
info@michaelandrewlaw.com
www.michaelandrewlaw.com

Selected publications

iEgoism by Michael Andrew Law
Softcover : 110 pages
Publisher : Xlibris LLC
ISBN: Softcover 978-1-4990-2124-0
ISBN: EBook 978-1-4990-2118-9

Michael Andrew Law The early years volume one: Nine Drawings from the early years collection
ISBN-10: 1503319407
ISBN-13: 978-1503319400

Michael Andrew Law The early years volume Two: Nine more Drawings from the early years collection (Volume 2)
ISBN-10: 1503365085
ISBN-13: 978-1503365087

Michael Andrew Law The early years volume Three: Nine Drawings from the early years collection (Volume 3)
ISBN-10: 1503366065
ISBN-13: 978-1503366060
Product Dimensions: 6 x 0.1 x 9 inches

Michael Andrew Law: Pale Hair Girls Catalogue (Volume 1)
Paperback: 124 pages
ISBN-10: 1503372111
ISBN-13: 978-1503372115
Product Dimensions: 8.5 x 0.3 x 8.5 inches

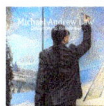

December To Remember: Michael Andrew Law Exhibition
Paperback: 120 pages
ISBN-10: 1505609259
ISBN-13: 978-1505609257

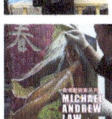

Hong Kong Artist Series: Michael Andrew Law 1
Paperback: 48 pages
ISBN-10: 1507580665
ISBN-13: 978-1507580660

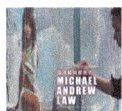

Hong Kong Artist Series: Michael Andrew Law 2'
Paperback: 48 pages
ISBN-10: 1507581556
ISBN-13: 978-1507581551

Michael Andrew Law

(852) 6444-7550
info@michaelandrewlaw.com
www.michaelandrewlaw.com

Publications : Illustrated Books

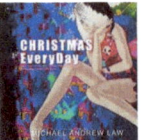

Christmas Everyday Book 1: Pale Hair Girls Christmas Series (Pale Hair Girls Christmas Everyday) (Volume 1)
ISBN-10: 1505453216
ISBN-13: 978-1505453218
Product Dimensions: 8.5 x 0.1 x 8.5 inches

Christmas Everyday Book 2: Pale Hair Girls Christmas Series (Pale Hair Girls Christmas Everyday) (Volume 2)
ISBN-10: 1505467799
ISBN-13: 978-1505467796
Product Dimensions: 8.5 x 0.1 x 8.5 inches

Christmas Everyday Book 3: Pale Hair Girls Christmas Series (Pale Hair Girls Christmas Everyday) (Volume 3)
ISBN-10: 1505468051
ISBN-13: 978-1505468052
Product Dimensions: 8.5 x 0.1 x 8.5 inches

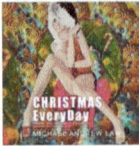

Christmas Everyday Book 4: Pale Hair Girls Christmas Series (Pale Hair Girls Christmas Everyday) (Volume 4)
ISBN-10: 1505470749
ISBN-13: 978-1505470741
Product Dimensions: 8.5 x 0.1 x 8.5 inches

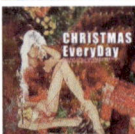

Christmas Everyday Book 5: Pale Hair Girls Christmas Series (Pale Hair Girls Christmas Everyday) (Volume 5)
ISBN-10: 1505470854
ISBN-13: 978-1505470857
Product Dimensions: 8.5 x 0.1 x 8.5 inches

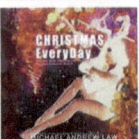

Christmas Everyday Book 6: Pale Hair Girls Christmas Series (Pale Hair Girls Christmas Everyday) (Volume 6)
ISBN-10: 150547115X
ISBN-13: 978-1505471151
Product Dimensions: 8.5 x 0.1 x 8.5 inches

Christmas Everyday: Special Edition (Pale Hair Girls Christmas Everyday) (Volume 7)
ISBN-10: 1505583926
ISBN-13: 978-1505583922
Product Dimensions: 8.5 x 0.3 x 8.5 inches

Michael Andrew Law

(852) 6444-7550
info@michaelandrewlaw.com
www.michaelandrewlaw.com

Selected Works for Art Events

iEgoism Exhibition at NatureArt ,Central District Hong Kong

iEgoism Exhibition In Photos (from left) : TV/ Movie stars Cherrie Kong ,Michael Andrew Law , Iva law ,Florence Lawman.

Michael Andrew Law exhibition at the Avenue of Stars, Hong Kong (星光大道).

Michael Andrew Law exhibition at the Avenue of Stars, Hong Kong (星光大道).

Art Related Events for Organic Beauty opening,

Art Talks at Credit Agricole CIB, Hong Kong Branch

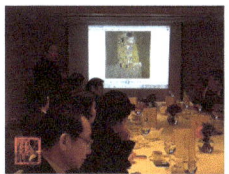

Art Talks for The Rotary Club of Hong Kong At The Peninsula Hong Kong

Michael Andrew Law

(852) 6444-7550
info@michaelandrewlaw.com
www.michaelandrewlaw.com

Selected Works for Art Events

As Guest Art Tutor at Diocesan Boys' School

Working With Film Producer & Founder of Hollywood Film Institute Dov Simens.

Art Competition Award ceremony with Dr. Sarah Mary Liao , then-Secretary for the Environment of the Hong Kong Special Administrative Region .

Self Curated Exhibition with Art Collectors at Art Center ,2005.

Curated Art Events with The Swire Group (太古集團).

Curated Art Events with Hong Kong Stock Exchange (香港交易所).

Michael Andrew Law

(852) 6444-7550
info@michaelandrewlaw.com
www.michaelandrewlaw.com

Art Event with Young Men's Christian Association (YMCA).

Group Exhibition, Hong Kong Convention and Exhibition Centre.

iEgoism Exhibition

Exhibition, Elements, Hong Kong

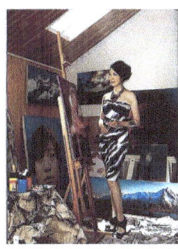

Oil Painting Shown in magazine :
壹周刊第1047期]第 20屆壹電視大獎 – 謝雪心

Michael Andrew Law

(852) 6444-7550
info@michaelandrewlaw.com
www.michaelandrewlaw.com

Selected Works for Art Events

Art Talk and Exhibition at Pui Shing Catholic Secondary School.

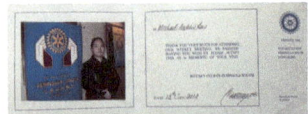

Art Talks and Charity Auction for The Rotary Club of Hong Kong At The Peninsula Hong Kong

Cardinal Zen Ze-kiun receives Michael Andrew Law at Ceremony. Comission portrait by Catholic Church of Hong Kong

Michael Andrew Law

(852) 6444-7550
info@michaelandrewlaw.com
www.michaelandrewlaw.com

The Pale Hair Universe Series

Medium : Traditional Oil Painting (With Acrylic Based) , Glitter , Gold Leaf .
About This Serie : Created Along with the First Series of painting of The Pale Hair Girls Original Series Paintings , Done with mixed media on canvas , with classical painting method.
Number of Paintings : 7 (As of 2015)
Availability : Limited Edition , Prints , Original Painting

Michael Andrew Law

(852) 6444-7550
info@michaelandrewlaw.com
www.michaelandrewlaw.com

Pale Hair Girls Original Series.

Medium : Traditional Oil Painting (With Acrylic Based) , Glitter , Gold Leaf .
About This Serie : First Series of painting of The entire Pale Hair Girls Universe ,
done with mixed media on canvas , with classical painting method.
Number of Paintings : 60 (As of 2015)
Availability : Limited Edition , Prints , Original Painting

Details

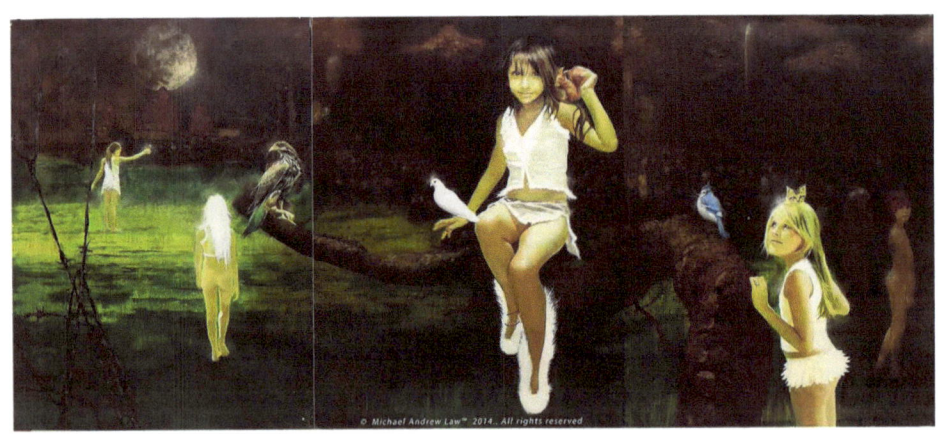

4'x 9' Multi-Panel Painting

info@michaelandrewlaw.com
www.michaelandrewlaw.com

Painting by Michael Andrew Law

30x20 ″ oil on canvas

S-P-R-I-N-G

info@michaelandrewlaw.com
www.michaelandrewlaw.com

© Michael Andrew Law™ 2014.All rights reserved

48x36 ˝ oil on canvas

Nothing stops dreams

info@michaelandrewlaw.com
www.michaelandrewlaw.com

© Michael Andrew Law™ 2014.All rights reserved

4'x 9' Multi-Panel Painting

info@michaelandrewlaw.com
www.michaelandrewlaw.com

© Michael Andrew Law™ 2014.All rights reserved

32x46 ˝ oil on canvas

Somewhere beyond my reach

36x48 ″ oil on canvas

Goodbye Future II

info@michaelandrewlaw.com
www.michaelandrewlaw.com

30x30 ˝ oil on canvas

I only dreams cause I am Alive.

info@michaelandrewlaw.com
www.michaelandrewlaw.com

Michael Andrew Law

(852) 6444-7550
info@michaelandrewlaw.com
www.michaelandrewlaw.com

Pale Hair Girls : The New

Medium : Mixed Media Painting (oil and Acrylic) , Glitter , Gold Leaf .
About This Serie : Second Series of painting of The entire Pale Hair Girls Universe ,
done with mixed media on canvas , classical method crossover with contemporary Digital painting method.
Number of Paintings : 80 (As of 2015)
Availability : Limited Edition , Prints , Special Edition .

Michael Andrew Law

(852) 6444-7550
info@michaelandrewlaw.com
www.michaelandrewlaw.com

Pale Hair Girls : The New

Medium : Mixed Media Painting (oil and Acrylic) , Glitter , Gold Leaf .
About This Serie : Second Series of painting of The entire Pale Hair Girls Universe ,
done with mixed media on canvas , classical method crossover with contemporary Digital
painting method.
Number of Paintings : 80 (As of 2015)
Availability : Limited Edition , Prints , Special Edition .

Michael Andrew Law

(852) 6444-7550
info@michaelandrewlaw.com
www.michaelandrewlaw.com

Pale Hair Girls : Christmas Everyday

Medium : Mixed Media Painting (digital print with Acrylic) , Glitter , Gold Leaf .
About This Serie : Special Series illustrations of The Pale Hair Girls Universe ,
done with mixed media on canvas , classical method crossover with contemporary Digital
painting method.
Number of Paintings : 102 (As of 2015)
Availability : Limited Edition , Prints , Special Edition .

Forgive the guilty.

am I allowed to go Christmas shopping?

Peace on earth will come to stay, when we live Christmas every day

How all of our hopes Had come down to this child

Michael Andrew Law

(852) 6444-7550
info@michaelandrewlaw.com
www.michaelandrewlaw.com

Pale Hair Girls : iEgoism

Medium : Mixed Media Painting (oil and Acrylic) , Glitter , Gold Leaf .
About This Serie : Third Series of painting of The entire Pale Hair Girls Universe ,
done with mixed media on canvas , classical method crossover with contemporary painting method.
Number of Paintings : 960 (As of 2015)
Availability : Limited Edition , Prints , Special Edition .

Michael Andrew Law

(852) 6444-7550
info@michaelandrewlaw.com
www.michaelandrewlaw.com

Pale Hair Girls : iEgoism

Medium : Mixed Media Painting (oil and Acrylic) , Glitter , Gold Leaf .
About This Serie : Third Series of painting of The entire Pale Hair Girls Universe ,
done with mixed media on canvas , classical method crossover with contemporary painting method.
Number of Paintings : 960 (As of 2015)
Availability : Limited Edition , Prints , Special Edition .

We ♥ MICHAEL ANDREW LAW

A Hong Kong contemporary artists

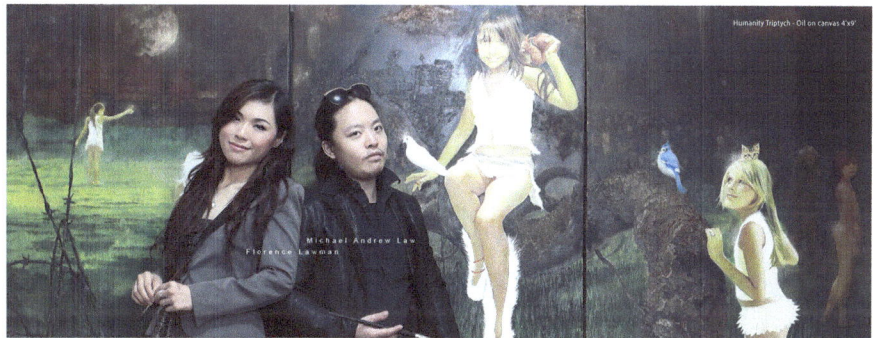

Humanity Triptych - Oil on canvas 4'x9'

Michael Andrew Law
Florence Lawman

Mr&Mrs.   Hong Kong Artist Couple

MICHAEL ANDREW LAW

八 十 後 香 港 藝 術 家 夫 婦

Most artists do not work as a couple, but many who do so succeed , such as Elaine & Williem De Kooning, Diego Rivera & Frida kahlo, Lee Krasner & Jackson Pollock, Franoise Gilot & Pablo Picasso, Georgia O'Keeffe & Alfred Stieglitz; artist couple are more than just working on artworks together, but its about the two artistic mind who have the deepest connection with each other , and take that power to make their biggest dreams ,come true.

Hong Kong homegrown artist **Michael Andrew Law** and **Florence Lawman** , both born into the 80s Pearl of the East Era of HongKong , growing up during the Pre and Post-handover decades, which was one of the most polarizing 30 years in Hong Kong history, with all the ups and downs in such a short period of time ; yet it also a time that needed Dreams more than ever ,Michael and Florence believe Art is the medium to makes dreams that can hold people together ,stay connected and happy.

Their works explore themes in a Generation Y perspective that characterizes the obsession with materialism and the vanity surrounding it . The archtectype is prevalent across Hong Kong pop culture since the 80s for what they grew up along with , from literature to movies , fashion , personal and social values .

Michael & Florence's works visually draws inspiration from Old Master's classical paintings by Caravaggio , Ruben , Rembrandt , tries to blend with Modern Art philosophy , inspired by Warhol , Murakami , Richter , De Kooning , Bacon , Wool and Prince .

Michael Andrew Law and **Florence Lawman** work , live in Hong Kong with their daughter Hermione.

Website : MichaelAndrewLaw.com
Contact :(+852) 6444-7850 / 6743-1317
LawManArt.com

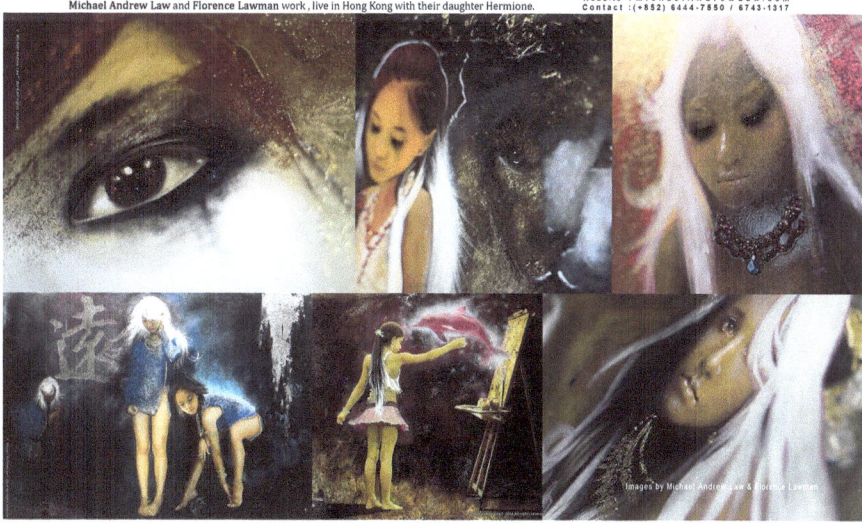

Images by Michael Andrew Law & Florence Lawman

Article from Hong Kong Art Magazines Art Plus and Art Map
March 2015 issues

Michael Andrew Law at Work.

Michael Andrew Law fusing digital and classical painting with west and East creative philosophy , to produce an extremely original artistic language and content that bridged west and east ,classical and modern medium , at the same time clearly tells the stories of his own generation. Combining digital creative materials and classical painting techniques with effusive yet knowing and precise focused , his paintings maintain a powerful tension between opposing aesthetic forces—expression and knowledge, control and spontaneity, savagery and wit, urbanity and primitivism—while providing satiric commentary on the oppressive realities of the predicament of Generation Internet, homegrown hongkonger's local-culture vesus Traditional Chinese culture, and The Hong Kong's post-handover history.

In his dynamically designed compositions, gracefully detailed figures and innocent faces are incise against fields that juxtaposed with portraits, chinese calligraphy, and sometimes cgi. The Pale Hair Girls Series (2006 - 2013) depicts realistic cold, icy-like young female figures surrounded by abstract and expressively painted forms and shapes revealing images of Pop culture, Historial figures, and Hong Kong landmarks.

Michael Andrew Law draws inspiration from Old Master's works such as Caravaggio , Ruben , Rembrandt , all the way to the Modern Art Superstars such as Warhol , Lichtenstein , Richter , De Kooning , Bacon , Wool and Prince . The Pale Hair Girls series mainly inspired by the painting works of French academic painter and traditionalist William-Adolphe Bouguereau and the Late Great YiFei Chen's characteristic "Romantic Realism" paintings.

In a reversal of standard East-West aesthetics, Law re-interprets Old Master's sophisticated imagery combine classical and digital materials—which resonate with Digital Vector Designs and Paintings—with fine strokes of oil paint multi-layered with paint film.In his interpretation of Leonardo Da Vinci's iconic Mona Lisa's smile (1517)—an iconic image that has been endlessly disseminated and reproduced—Law painted over the symbolism of the portrait Mona Lisa with his young wife , intent on rendering the figure in contemporary fashion with the iconic image as background .

"The Humanity triptych" depicts New Generation HongKongers in a Ruined Hong Kong city , awaiting their unknown fate of a new beginning. This painting series explores one of the central paradox of his art—between romance and derision , his romantic magnanimity as an artist and his pessimistic perspective on the predicament of Generation Y Hongkongers. Here, this paradox is symbolized by the stark contrast of icy cold young female and disturbing representations of the armageddon-like of images. Whether portrayed as single "chinese calligraphy " or in triptych composition and classical paintwork that combine both expressive and traditional painting techniques with the digital vector , the beauties and the human figures stand as eternal motifs in the history of art and also in popular culture. Both oppositional and parallel, they are reminders of the fragile vibrancy of life and the impitoyable passing of time.

A references between different cultural refrence (high/pop, classical/contemporary, east/west), Michael Andrew Law has stated that an artist should be someone who understood how to hybrid between different worlds and go ahead makes an effort to knowing them. With his distinctive "iEgoism" philosophy , which employs highly refined academic painting techniques to depict a mixture of abstract expressionism within a representational pop culture images. These techniques parallel to the themes of romance and predicament of this generation , he recollects and revitalizes narratives of irony and introspection.

Michael Andrew Law was born in 1982 in British Hong Kong , studied fine art with american artist Daniel Anderson and with artist graduatee of China Central Academy of Fine Arts Sam Zeng from 2003 - 2006 . He co-founded the Hong Kong Art Studio Nature Art Workshop in 2008. In addition to the production and marketing of Michael Andrew Law's art and related work, Nature Art functions as a supportive environment for the
fostering of emerging Hong Konger artists. Law is also a curator. In 2013, he organized an exhibition of contemporary art titled "iEgoism ," which served as a commentaries of contemporary HongKong Gen Y pop culture ;These Theroy also published in the book : "ïEgoism" in 2014.

Michael Andrew Law currently works and lives in Hong Kong.

2010 Avenue of Stars, Hong Kong
Exhibition :

2013 DeTour Matters 2013 Satellite Events at NatureArt Gallery
2013 December to Remember , One man show at NatureArt Gallery Central District, Hong Kong.
2012 Solo Show , Park Central tseung kwan O ,Hong Kong
2011 Art Walk Group Showing , Discovery Bay ,Hong Kong
2011 HK Gold Coast (Book signing exhibition)
2009 Solo Painting Exhibition The Avenue of Stars
Group Exhibition of Daniel Anderson workshop Classical Realism class of 2008 at Manhattan,NY
2007 Guest and ExhibitionThe Peak Galleria Hong Kong
2007 Invited workshop exhibition, Elements, Hong Kong
Group Exhibition of Classical Realism class of 2007 at Manhattan,NY
2006 Collection by Cardinal Zen Ze-kiun and exhibited at Catholic Church of Hong Kong.
2004 - 2007, Hong Kong Young Artist Group Exhibition, Hong Kong Central Library.
Group Exhibition of Classical Realism class of 2006 at East Village, Manhattan,NY
2005 illustration original exhibition for Kung Kao Po
2004 Group Exhibition, Wanchai Tower
2003 Group Exhibition, Hong Kong Convention and Exhibition Centre,
2003 Winner of I luv Hong Kong Painting Competition, exhibition at The Landmark (Hong Kong).
2002 The Holy story Picture Book illustrated picture original exhibition ,sai wan ho civic centre.

SELECTED COLLECTIONS :

Cardinal of the Catholic Church Joseph Zen Ze-kiun
Organic Beauty Inc
Agriculture, Fisheries and Conservation Department
Ms.Ho Wei Ying
Ms. Annie Yu
Daniel Anderson
MR.Tsang Yan Sam

PUBLICATIONS :

Fisheye magazine , featured artist interview , November 2002
Kung Kao Po , interview , June 2006
Art of Rock Realism , 2008
The Art of Michael Andrew Law , 2010
December to Remember One man Show Art Book , 2013
iEgoism , 2015

Solo Shows 2010 - 2013

I really appreciate your purchase of this Painting

Collection Book , I hope you enjoy reading them as

much as I enjoyed painting them!

May God bless your home with peace, joy and love.

From Michael Andrew Law.

Find Me Online.

Michael Andrew Law Q

www.ingramcontent.com/pod-product-compliance
Lightning Source LLC
Chambersburg PA
CBHW050827180526
45159CB00004B/1817